THE INSOMNIAC DRAGON
POEMS

Kraftgriots

Also in the series (POETRY)

Sunday Okpanachi: *A Song for Inikpi*
Ada Ugah: *Colours of the Rainbow*, winner, 1991 Association of Nigerian Authors (ANA) poetry prize.
David Cook et al: *Rising Voices*
Sesan Ajayi: *A Burst of Fireflies*
Akomaye Oko: *Clouds*
Olu Oguibe: *A Gathering Fear*, winner, 1992 All Africa Okigbo prize for Literature & Honourable mention, 1993 Noma Award for Publishing in Africa.
Nnimmo Bassey: *Patriots and Cockroaches*
Okinba Launko: *Dream-Seeker on Divining Chain*
Onookome Okome: *Pendants*; winner, 1993 ANA/Cadbury poetry prize
Uba Ofei: *Beyond Fear and Fury*
Abiodun Ehindero: *Response of the Dead*
Uba Ofei: *After the Fire*
Nnimmo Bassey: *Poems on the Run*
Ebereonwu: *Suddenly God was Naked*
Tunde Olusunle: *Fingermarks*
Joe Ushie: *Lambs at the Shrine*
Chinyere Okafor: *From Earth's Bedchamber*
Ezenwa Ohaeto: *The Voice of the Night Masquerade;* joint winner, 1997 ANA/Cadbury poetry prize
George Ehusani: *Fragments of Truth*
Remi Raji: *A Harvest of Laughters;* joint-winner, 1997 ANA/Cadbury poetry prize.
Patrick Ebewo: *Self-Portrait & Other Poems*
George Ehusani: *Petals of Truth*
Nnimmo Bassey: *Intercepted*
Joe Ushie: *Eclipse in Rwanda*
Femi Oyebode: *Selected Poems*
Ogaga Ifowodo: *Homeland & Other Poems,* winner, 1993 ANA poetry prize
Godwin Uyi Ojo: *Forlorn Dreams*
Tanure Ojaide: *Delta Blues and Home Songs*
Tony Nwazuoke: *Windows of Life*
Niyi Osundare: *The Word is an Egg* (2000)
Tayo Olafioye: *A Carnival of Looters* (2000)
Ibiwari Ikiriko: *Oily Tears of the Delta* (2000)
Francis A. Odiniya: *The Traveller with Two Souls* (2000)
Arnold Udoka: *I am the Woman* (2000)
Akinloye Ojo: *In Flight* (2000)
Joe Ushie: *Hill Songs* (2000)

THE INSOMNIAC DRAGON
POEMS

Ebereonwu

Published by

Kraft Books Limited
6A Polytechnic Road, Sango, Ibadan
Box 22084, University of Ibadan Post Office
Ibadan, Oyo State, Nigeria
☏ 234 (02) 8106655
Email: krabooks@skannet.com

© Ebereonwu 2000

First published 2000

ISBN 978-039-035-9

=KRAFTGRIOTS=
(A literary imprint of Kraft Books Limited)

All Rights Reserved

First printing, November 2000

Computer typeset by GLJ General Services Ltd., Ibadan

Printmarks Ventures, Ososami, Ibadan.

Dedication
Come oh birds of the air
That neither sow nor reap
Feed on the fruit of my labour
And lend wings to my thoughts

Contents	Page
Dedication	5
Just a poet	9
Palace of roses	10
The reminder	11
Golden wreath	12
The vengeance of ken	13
Song of the insomniac	14
Guess what's on the menu?	16
Next door	17
Sixty-six beginning	18
Mankind	19
Of Rubies and topaz	21
Garuba's sonnet	22
Baptism of fire	23
Born soldier	24
Who goes there?	25
The call	26
Noah's disappointment	27
Primordial tongue	28
Under the bushel	29
Witching time	30
Taj mahal	31
The puritan	32
Across the globe	33
Upon a barren fig	34
Tales beneath	35
Question quest	36
Checkmate safari	37
Fated journey	38
Flight of the wingless bird	39
Raining	40
Animal attraction	41
A prophesie	42
Non-stop harmony	43
The rain-maker	44

Deep pit	45
Behind closed doors	46
Skyward gaze	47
Bereaved of herself	48
Son of the dragon	49
The beautiful one	50
Sleep ecstasy	51
Metaphorique	52
Soul mate	53
Sage	54
Laughing matter	55
Dateline africa	56
Shattered remains	57
The sower	58
At last	59
Goodbye day	60

Just a poet

A man extricates himself
From the grip of reality
And protects his head
With a helmet of cloud

He is a poet
His views are shadows
Conceived in colours
His grip on reality
Is sketched in a void

I am just a poet
Sketching in a void
A vanity for eternity
My eyes are two moons
That sparkle at noon
My voice is the muteness
That echoes in an abyss
My poetry is the graffiti
On the trunk of a jacaranda.

Palace of roses

Erect a shelter
Upon my sorrows
Let it be called
The grand palace

Set my dinner
On a marble table
And let me dine
With a golden spoon

Lend me a tailor
From god of needle
To stitch my regalia
With a silver thread

Take me on a visit
To queen of Sheba
Get me her princess
To be my bride

Sing us a lullaby
With chords of harp
And make us sleep
On my bed of roses

Wake me up
On Monday morning
And please tell me
It will be alright.

The reminder

Because of porridge
You sold the chair
Meant to remind you
That they have stolen your buttocks
Now you cannot still sit
Now not a morsel is left.

When next the melody of your agony
Touches my sympathetic heart
I will recline in my own chair
And teach the children to dance.

Golden wreath

In your coming
Is good tiding

In your presence
Is an essence

But your eyes
Hold an ice

And your pocket
Hides a bucket

Of a bottomless depth
To be filled with gem
Stolen from the mine
Of wealth of a nation

In your plunder
You created hunger

In your whims
You trailed victims

In your might
You spurned myth

In you demise
I found muse

The golden wreath
Upon your grave
Is a bowl of spittle
From my golden teeth.

The vengeance of ken

    Smile
    You who loves death
    It is now on your door

In hell the gate widens
A special furnace is wrought
And the fire made hotter
To warm a beloved son

On earth the knees are bent
As ordinary mortals give thanks
To Him that promised to visit
The sin of the father on son

    Oh
    What a sad news
    That gladdens the heart

Glory glory to the Most High
Such event as happened today
Reaffirm the faith of a people
On the efficacy of ill-wishes

    Smile
    You who loves death
    S-M-I-L-E.

Song of the insomniac

From the land beyond
The voice of my fathers
Burst forth into particles
Shooting up to the sky
And down into the sea
Hovering the atmosphere
To move my lips

I sing of vultures
And dogs and rats
It is not a song
That sways the trees
Or makes stars dance
It is not my song
That creates waves

At the funeral rites
I sing to the vulture
He will never look young
Till he stops making meal
Out of putrid flesh

Deaf to intimidating barking
I sing to the dog
He will always be in chains
Till he stops wagging tail
For his oppressors favour

Down into the holes
I sing to the rat
He will never stop hiding
Till he denounces larceny
Light will always be tortuous

I will sing of putrid flesh
Chains and holes in the psyche
And if I will sing of you
I will not sing sweet songs
Or like the caged bird praises
My song is the lullaby
That engenders insomnia
My song wakes up the night.

Guess what's on the menu?

The blind rat that stole my fish
Unaware of the trap becomes a dish

I have never had something as good
Or better than this in a long month

So delicious is sour broth
To a famished mouth

But the rat resurrects in my stomach
A radical with revolutionary ideas

Upsetting conventional metabolism
Cursing initiating an uprising

There is now an emergency
To be diagnosed in the toilet

Prof, what can you teach a pauper
That he has not learnt from hunger?

Next door

My teeth are not fangs
Neither are my hands claws
My nails are no razor
And my spittle not venom

But don't call me a good man

I can neither hurt a fly
A spider or even a gecko
Mosquitoes nestle on my pond
My tears feed the thirsty fish

But don't call me a good man

I have drowned a river in the ocean
And buried the night in the dark
I am my parents unrealized ambition
My lover's promise never to be fulfilled

So don't call me a good man

I am a pregnant coin in a leprous pocket
The spectre that haunts a gossipy street
I am the zero multiplied a million times
The sin that begs not for forgiveness

So don't call me a good man
I am the temple of the idle mind.

Sixty-six beginning

Tomorrow I will be sixty-six
With as much number of regrets
And more past and less future
Constant sigh is my anniversary song

Who will share with me this moment
Who will dance for me with one leg

Mules carry burdens to the mountains
Birds from the valleys bring back memories
It is a thousand years ago youth departed
Sorrows now pilgrim on the ruin of my being

Who will share with me this burden
Who will tell my tale to the hills

If I put on an anticlockwise watch
Impress my footstep on a rewind button
And reread the milestone backward
I return where the beginning began

But in the dwelling place of the past
No passages opening into the future

So as wings of thought take flight
My teeth dancing in their sockets
Desert and oasis grey and bald
I stoop celebrating on three legs

For the future less to count and regret
But more important to live till end.

Mankind

I have transversed the world
On the back of a vampire
Rode on the belly of a whale
To visit the maiden of the ocean
Fetched firewood from fiery forest
My escort was king lion himself

>In the heart of a flea
>Lives the rest of us
>With our gifts and rewards
>To offer the highest bidder
>And curses and ill-wishes
>To whom we cannot exploit

I bandaged the arm of a wounded lion
And lent my trousers to the monkey
With which he visits his in-laws
I was the maestro of universal eminence
Trained to tame the tarantula's temper
But a salty river coursed from my eyes

>For I fear fellow man
>Hiding evil in cosmetic face
>Smiling with five fingers
>Extended for a handshake
>While in his embrace
>Throbs the pulse of malevolence

The cobra's venom was my cough syrup
While the nightingale taught me to sing
I have climbed the peak of Kilmanjaro
On the wisdom of a mountain goat
There's no track too tough to tackle
After experiencing speed with a cheetah

But I am in a race
Against the rest of us
And there is no hope
Of victory peace or joy
Until I breast the tape
In my forefather's bosom

I can transverse the earth
On the back of a vampire
But peace with fellow man
Is in the heart of the unborn.

Of rubies and topaz

Away from rubies and topaz
To escape into the wilderness
The vast landscape of my mind
Searching for the self to discover

I have seen living dinosaurs
Present in their frozen future
I have visited nightmares
Before they maraud my sleep

Out there is heaven and hell
Filled rooms in need of tenants
Saints and serpents with scriptures
Clamouring to tempt attention

I am alone and in solace
Other visions distract from mine
Company offered privacy ruined
Destination reached target missed

A priceless gem fallows inside
The stream of the subconscious
I light a lamp and prospect
For the I only I can recognize

And here a snapshot of tomorrow
I will be alone and in company
When true self sparkles infinite
Away from rubies and topaz.

Garuba's sonnet

Garuba I have heard what you said
No need to visit enchanted lands
To procure the necessary evidence
No need to invite silent shadows
To vouch for your integrity

To make a tragic news lose its sting
Sometimes a poet's craft is inadequate
Where truth weighs like a dead elephant
A higher genius may improvise the lever
To hoist it upon delicate shoulders

So Garuba I have heard what you said
No need to resurrect your ancestors
To corroborate your statement
No need to quote St. John.

Baptism of fire

How did fire get its name
By melting metals boiling waters
Keeping the night at arms lent
Or scaring the cold away

The kettle smeared black
Would prefer a different name
Unlike fire in a lamp
Is endearingly called light

Fire was not christened by the tortoise
That fled its safe carapace
And screamed into River Jordan
When fire caught its tail

In the garden of friction
Fire flowers a sprinkly spark
A hand scalded in the process
Learns the opposite of pleasure

Fire is the colour of rage
Irons mate to beget thunder
Fire is the father of smokes
All the clouds are kinsmen

What burns in the heart is passion
What dances on the stove flame
Not the bullet expelled by a trigger
What burns so wild is rumour

Fire is the infant cry
Of an excited thunder.

Born soldier

In the beginning was a man
Looking for a woman
He is a bachelor

In the middle was a woman
Looking for a child
She is a spinster

In the end was a child
Looking for a man
He is a storm

Born with his boots on
In the house that Jack built
In the centre of the battlefield

Who goes there?

Who goes there
Bag bulging with barrage of ideas
Words cannot adequately express
To release the untapped resources
Caged by linguistic tyranny

Who goes there
Attacking the tombs of dead words
Exhuming their dry bones and
Breathing a new flesh into them
To contest space with existing ones

Who goes there
In defiance of dictionary definitions
With cannon poised to blast down
Age long traditions of grammar
Anarchy crawling on papyrus

     Who goes there?
     Who goes there!
     A poet, sir.

The call

I heard my name in the wild
The leopard is calling me
Caught in the undergrowth
A snare drains his blood

I heard my name in the village
The hunter is calling
Caught in a vicious circle
Hunger ravages his hut

Then I heard my name again
In the wild in the village
The hunter is calling me
The leopard is calling me.

Noah's disappointment

He told me about the vision
But I was mired in dirt
So I wanted to have a shower

Then he began to build the Ark
The allure of a maiden beckons
And I wanted to have a shower

When he completed its building
I was the first he invited in
But I wanted to have a shower

Then he withdrew anchor and set sail
40 day and 40 night it did not rain
And I wanted to have a shower.

Primordial tongue

It has been hours too long
And your silence reverberates
Against the wall of my passion

The rain rattling on the roof
Singing a tune for two
Your silence drowns the rain song

Tongue tied lips sealed
Voice stilled mouth locked
Speech moving on a tiptoe

Can only be seen with the eyes
But a man blinded by desire
I touch words that I see

There is a primordial tongue
I share with every beast
Grunts and squirms are alphabets

In the true spelling of response
So whatever you want to say
Do not say it in English

A man convulsed by desire
I share a tribe with the beast.

Under the bushel

Inside a hole I lived
Awaiting the moment
You will walk by
And I shall look up
To impress my sight
With a view of the promise land
Which I may not enter
To catch a glimpse
Of the forbidden fruit
That shades my garden
But not quench my thirst

In respite of sleep
You went by unseen
But the serpent awoke
Pointed to the direction
Of your fading scent
And under the bushel
I saw you beckoned
I approached unafraid of reproach
And you took my hand in yours
And led me unto the grass bed

Here the trees shed no leaves
To cover our stark nakedness
And flowers dedicate their bloom
To those who probe for nectar.

Witching time

Let there be light
And there was blackout
Man-made night, imposed moment
The eyes of the sun blindfolded

I look into the mirror
The face of darkness stares back
And if I scream in terror
My neighbours will fall asleep
They relish the aroma of dusk
The grunge of nocturnal rites

A dark banner kidnaps daylight
Noon is born in night's image
And not a wink from the sun
While we grope and blunder
The candle of our destiny
Suffocates without a glow

Let there be light I scream
My neighbours wriggle their ears
Deep in their slumber
They listen to the owl sing.

Taj mahal

A man who perceives that
Living in a skyscraper makes him
Taller than those in a hut
Is not wrong

But must believe that
Those living in Greenland
Are greener than natives of Blackburn
To be right

Not all in Taj Mahal are royals
Not where a man goes in to
That defines him Jesus said
But what he comes out with

There is a fool in every city
Even in the highest heaven
There must be an angel
Who did not pass Mathematics

It takes a twine to take the mountain
And with ladder can touch the roof
But ropes staircases elevators combined
No man succeeds beyond his mentality.

The puritan

Those two shameless dogs
Why are they joined
Together back to back
This early morning

By the way
Don't they know
Today is Sunday.

Across the globe

Remove your dress
At the statue of liberty
Donate your bra
To Venus de Milo
Hang your pants
On the Wall of China
Lay your back
On the bed of Amazon
Spread your legs
Across the equator
Call my name
And crave for heaven
The spear of Chaka
Will pierce your warmth.

Upon a barren fig

Lay not your axe upon a barren fig
It is the sanctuary of nestling birds
Botanical haven to nurture their likes
A squirrel's bunker when the falcon strikes

Lay not your wrath upon a barren fig
Idling on the way of the weary wayfarer
Her arms spread an umbrella against
The grinning sun and its seething angst

In dew the medicine man pays homage
Her roots and barks she offers generously
When the sun sets he concocts an elixir
To shoo ailments and make life easier

Upon a barren fig lay not your axe
Your wrath your venom your curse
Night hardly comes to favour a witch
Nor a fig bloom to frustrate your wish.

Tales beneath

There is an earth beneath this earth
Beyond the kingdom of Anthill
Where the deepest root cannot touch
And the oldest moon spins no yarn

Dive heading from tree top
Plunge into a lazy lake
Confront a stammering storm
And doze without waking up

You will be there beneath the earth
Where the seas are buried
Earth treasures embalmed
The homeland of fables

Without flesh blood and bone
You will meet your fathers
Weaving muse on spider thread
Beings without structure

Losing all human forms
You will be changed into a fairy
And if you love stories
You will be turned into a parable

Told along the narrow pathway
Through the seven sleeping seas
Beyond the palace of the ant queen
Inside a fairy tale beneath the earth.

Question quest

When a dog thinks itself a tiger
When a skunk labels its odour fragrance
There are questions never to be asked

A kid asks: Mama from where did I come
A shove on the head postpones a reply
There are questions better answered by time

Never ask a whore the father of her child
Never ask a vulture where he got his hair cut
Never ask a drunk where he lost his hat

When blooming rabbits germinate on a carrot farm
When two plus four puts the account in red
The joy of subtraction reaches an anticlimax

There is a question a deaf never asks a blind
An answer a clergy never reveals to the flock
Inside every coconut dwells a stranded lake

The thirty-two differences between zero and nil
Are best discovered by an inward quest
For every mystery an answer sleeps in the mind

When a dead man pretends to be asleep
When a rat on a cat's claw smiles
An answer is asking a question.

Checkmate

Tonight
The leopard called
The gazelle answered
In silence

Oh tonight
The cat with nine lives
The rat with nine holes
Will outlive each other.

Fated journey

I think I have reached my destination
The graveyard where differences are buried
But I am waiting for the car to stop
For the driver to apply the brake
For the brake mechanism to function well

Beloved I have no hold on the future
My hands are circled round your neck
Spreading the handkerchief for the tears
Sweat and snort that will be embalmed
When this vehicle is driven into a ditch

It is your lot to give the command
Not to inflate the tyres with tirades
We have almost gone past spots of hope
The next corner opens to the labyrinth
Where our personae will lose each other

Then this long sentence makes no meaning
If the fullstop is applied by a ditch.

Flight of the wingless bird

Out of the grave
A mustard jumped up
And kissed the sun

A wingless bird flew
Across an astonished sky
On the wings of a storm

A midget hung his hat
On the tallest tree
A hill on his heel

And I will twinkle
With the stars
When the night sings.

Raining

It is raining
    Cat and dog
Asleep on the manger
    Cat and dog
Baying and purring
    Cat and dog
Canine and feline
    Cat and dog
Toothache and Paw Paw
    Cat and dog
Catalogue and dogma
    Cat and dog
It is raining
    Cat and dog.

Animal attraction

The eyes of an owl, my grandpa counselled
Will see you through the dark tunnel
Never taste the head of a cockerel
Else you will crow before your sun sets

A plate of fish fin, the old one advised
First thing before commencing a journey
In case your boat runs into a storm
You will swim safely out of troubled water

A dish of money paw, grandpa insisted
Will help you climb to higher heights
The horns of a gazelle to your visitors
And they will blow your trumpet always

> I have carried a mule
> Barked at a dog
> Stung a scorpion
> And croaked at a toad

But the odd wheel of misfortune
Still played a mischievous trick on me
And there is no smoke in my kitchen
No wood no weed no seed in the barn

Grandpa, when did I eat this iguana
That turned my skin dry and scaly?

A prophesie

By the time
It will come to pass
From me
You will hear no more

Take heed
That you may not stray
From this event
That will come our way

It is
Neither fortune nor curse
But
Rather a part of us

The land
Shall be like chalk
The people
Shall be like chalk

Son of my mother
Think back to days before and before
Child of my mother
Remember the Ibos knew no king.

Non-stop harmony

The night is going to be long
Check your strings one more time
Let there be no cause for discord
Sit the best seat in comfort
And in the interest of harmony
Play your banjo real good
Like you have never done before

We have come from distant lands
Arriving here before the morning sun
Flaming noon has come and gone
Salty sweat has drained and dried
Patiently we have waited and waited
The night is going to be long
And your rhythm will soothe our nerves

So in the interest of harmony
Play your banjo real good maestro
And do not demand for a fee.

The rain-maker

The rainbow kissed the earth
Where the rainman laid his egg
Decorated with garlands the whirlwind
Twirled in prodigal delight

The living colour is stripped off the greens
Sprouting chaffs where crops were planted
No moisture on the lips of the earth
The fiery sun is drunk with vapour

With these situations on mind
He set about the three stones
And with a bellow made fire
Which he muffled with leaves

Out emerges the envoy smoke
Which ascends with the message
Soon the storm gathers trees tremble
Two thousand rays or a sun flee

When the clouds heed the rainman's call
The skirts worn by the days ahead
Will be products of a wet loom.

Deep pit

Tort the toiseman dropped
Into a pit full of shit
He shouted for help
Nobody heard him
He could not climb
So he accepted his fate

On the seventh day
His son made a discovery
"Papa, are you there?"
Yeah, Tort growled in reply
"Just a moment, Papa
While I get the ladder."

Hurry up son, Tort screamed
Hurry up quickly and fast
The smell of shit
Is suffocating me!

---

*Adapted from an Ibo folktale

Behind closed doors

She is a house of doors
Doors behind and on backside
And I have always entered
Through the straightaway front

But when flowers wither so soon
On a path trodden always
The search for lost fragance
Is taken beyond closed options

Knock knock on next time
Bend low and open the door
I enter from the back

Skyward gaze

I sat on a chair with my head
Looking at the wind with my toes
And the chair wanted to know why

A meteor zoomed through the window
Of my open door into the blue oblivion
Its flight route immortalized on the sky

But if I sit with my buttocks
I will never know the point
Where the kite overtakes the wind

And if the moon counts days
I shall sum up the constellation
Now that my gaze is celestial

But how can I explain all these
When the chair has not told me
Why it sits on the earth with four legs.

Bereaved of herself

On the rope
Was her own corpse
She saw it herself

Lonely in the midst of company
Thirsty at the bank of a river
Mourning on the day of birth
Unmoved by the sound of music
Cold to the touch of tenderness

She stared at the sun
She stared and stared
And stared at the sun

Guilty without an offence
Angry at the words of humour
Repulsed by the fragrance of rose
Numb to the delicacy of taste
Melancholic in spite of victory

Hanging on the rope again
This is the third time
She has committed suicide.

Son of the dragon

Man originates from Adam
Even fathers and undertakers
I am of course a lion
Claws mane and growl
With a six foot long tail
But mother is a dragon
That is why I breathe fire
And have some extra heads
To tidy up the floor

Thunder and lightning
In shapes and genetics
Are my blood brothers
Children of my mother
We dream same dreams
Centipedes and leonines
Are my blood brothers
Children of my parents
We resemble ourselves

Share many things in common
In size and in character
Flying in soils and jungles
Swimming in stars and papers
Inhabiting the atmosphere
Claws of tail and fire
Union of lion and dragon
Every man is from Adam
Every man. Not even I.

The beautiful one

Though your hair is covered
By your hairscarf
I know it is beautiful

Though your breasts are covered
By your bra and blouse
I know they are beautiful

Though your majesty is covered
By your pants and skirt
I know it is beautiful

I can see your legs
They are not covered
They are not beautiful.

Sleep ecstasy

All alone in a lonely night
I close my eyes it's you I see
I kiss your lips I bite my teeth
I open my eyes you disappear

Amaze me no more with your maze
Of angles triangles and rectangles
Turning me around and running around
I walk homeward with no reward

All alone in a lonely sleep
The bed squeaks I hear you moan
You run your fingers around my body
You scratch my back and light a fire

Passion heated to such fahrenheit
Creates a leeway for its vapour
All my sweet desires of you
I will fulfil in my dreams

     It is raining now
     In my sleep ecstasy
     Only my pyjama is soaked.

Metaphorique

Two things look alike
One is beautiful
The other ugly

Day life is night death
In the blindman's sight
Night and day are same

Lies and silence are same
Either tells not the truth
Silence is a golden lie

Nightlife is death day
Life is death reversed
We die to live to die

However anyway in fact
Therefore no matter what
Cry no more woman

Tears and salt are same
Salt is the tears in the
Blue eyes of the ocean

However anyway the fact is
We live to die to live
Therefore cry no more woman

The dead are living
The dead are dying
The dead are crying for us.

Soul mate

Dread in the heart
Storm in the hair
Rastafari I

Birds on his lock
Mom saw mom saw
Picking off lice

He is crazy
He is lazy
What a lie

Whiff of wee
Contains seven books
Now I realize

Green gold rhythm
Red black soul
In his arm I'll die

Yeah mom!

Sage

Answers answers
He knew it all
He said it all
He tried it all
It all failed

Horizontally vertically
The sage was foolish
Very very foolish.

Laughing matter

Draw back your jaw
Separate the thick lips
Let the shining sun
Reflect on your enamel

Release the sound
Of ha-ha-ha
That will echo
Joy in your heart
Soothe away sorrows
Repelling steam of stress

Rejoice and rejoice
Chorus the songbird's song
Its melody caresses nature
Brings forth good tidings

Ha ha ha
Apply supply multiply it
Even when you are sad
Rejoice seriously
Do not joke with laughter.

Dateline africa

Sunday is the day for angels and virgins
Unseen and unsinned they beget sons of men
As I carry my cross to the pawn merchant

Monday: The day slavery began
Back on the trans-saharan route
My turn to sell my ancestors

Tuesday not recognized by kopernicus
A map wrongly drawn incubates in a mine
From broken shells is hatched a hero's lore

> A child is born today
> To no one in particular
> His name is Wednesday

Thursday: The birthday of the grandest grandpa
Who gave out his rib and was sold an apple
Now you have seen your nakedness grandpa

> Friday worship at the shrine
> To the beat of afrorhythm
> For eternity lives Africa

Saturday - shorter than the twelfth hour
The sun of this land illuminates other lands
Take heart Africa your sun will shine again.

Shattered remains

The roach and I
Discovered daylight
Inside a poultry

The roach grew grey
And became a hen
The hen became me

Then what is in me
That makes a man
Claim I am him

I of borrowed components
Hen roach and whatever
Is in whatever in them

The him in me but
The micro swimmer
That lost its head

Shadows share traits
With darkness but
Are children of light

God gave me soul
The elements the body
Joined to genetic codes

And if sleep goes forever
Jah receives my soul
Body returns to elements

What remains thereafter
A dismembered history
In a shattered mirror.

The sower

On the land under his feet
Which inhales and exhales life
He sows brown beans and melon

On the valley which cuddles the sun
Maize cassava and fruited pumpkin
On the goat farm he plants milk

In the night when the sky is blue
She comes searching for butterflies
And he sows in her garden
The seed of the unfolding dawn.

At last

It must either be the vultures
Or the creatures of the seas
Else the burrowing cretins
Will have me for a feast

But if I am served on a pyre
And is devoured by a blaze
And is defecated as ash
In my grandmother's garden

That tree that flower
That okra that ripe tomato on
The evening market basket
Will all be my resurrection.

Goodbye day

On the day of my convocation
I pray you will be there
To witness the final moment
When I will embrace the big guest
And pass out with a smile

If by normal circumstance
You were late to the occasion
Perhaps family matters caused the delay
Or the traffic jam held you up
And you arrived when tears were flowing
And friends and foes were singing praises
Never regret the moment you had missed

But I wished you were there
On that day of my convocation
To witness the final moment
When I embraced the big guest
And passed out with a smile

If you called out my sweet name
And I did not answer you
And you read this lovely poem
And I did not make a comment
And you threw a challenge
And I did not spring up
Know you then I have said bye

To you to everybody everything
In this wonder school of life
Those I know those I could not
Take good care of yourselves

Never forget the lesson you missed
One day it will be your turn
Bye.

www.ingramcontent.com/pod-product-compliance
Lightning Source LLC
Chambersburg PA
CBHW070338230426
43663CB00011B/2365